I0559711

Mom Needs A Day Off

Sylvia G. Alston

An Imprint of Journal Joy Publishers

Copyright © 2025 by Sylvia Alston

An Imprint of Journal Joy Publishers

All rights reserved and printed in the United States of America. No part of this book may be reproduced, distributed, or transmitted in any form or by any means, without the authors' prior written permission, except in the case of brief quotations embodied in critical reviews and specific other noncommercial uses permitted by copyright law.

For Publishing Information, contact Journal Joy at Info@thejournaljoy.com.
www.thejournaljoy.com

Paperback ISBN: 978-1-957751-87-0
Ebook ISBN: 978-1-957751-88-7
Editor: Khalia Tarver

First paperback edition, 2025

Dedication

My first book is dedicated to my mother, who sacrificed so much of her life so that I could write this book and become an author.
Mom, you raised a success story!

Secondly, to every mother who has ever felt overwhelmed with motherhood but wouldn't change being a mom for anything in the world—this book is not just for children to understand that "Mom needs a day off." It's also a reminder for mothers to take time for self-care.

Your forever happiness outweighs your right-now happiness. Be kind to yourself.

Lastly, I dedicate this book to all the children I've had the pleasure of teaching. Each of you holds a special place in my heart.

S. G. Alston

I'm going to school but my mom said she has the day off.

It started off like a normal morning. I got out of bed, brushed my teeth, and put my clothes on.

My mom was combing my hair when she said, "I'm taking the day off."

"Mom? What does it mean—taking the day off?"

"You know how sometimes you get tired and take a nap at school?

Well, mommies don't get to take naps, so mommies get really tired."

"What are you tired from?"

"Well, while everyone is still sleeping, I wake up, do laundry, fix breakfast, pack lunches, check my work emails, and lay your clothes out."

"Then, when you wake up, I help you get dressed, comb your hair, and help you get ready for school."

"I drop you off at school, then Mommy goes to work."

"What do you do at work, Momma?"

"Momma goes to a lot of meetings and talks to people all day."

"Do you like your job?"

"Yes. I get to meet lots of new people."

"Does your job make you tired?"

"Sometimes."

"Is that why you are taking the day off?"

"Yes, I'm taking the day off to rest and take a nap."

"I'm going to go to the spa, the coffee shop, and lunch."

"When can I get a day off?"

"Soon, baby. Soon."

ABOUT THE AUTHOR
SYLVIA ALSTON

Sylvia G. Alston, affectionately known as "Syl" by her family and friends, is a children's book author and dedicated educator in the field of Early Childhood Education. Born in our nation's capital, Washington, D.C., and raised in Prince George's County, Maryland, Sylvia has always had a passion for reading and nurturing young children.

She holds an Associate degree in Psychology and a Bachelor's degree in Criminal Justice from the University of Phoenix, and she is currently pursuing a Master of Education degree at Walden University.

Sylvia's journey in early childhood education began at the age of 16, when she worked at a childcare center during the summer. It was then she discovered her God-given gift for working with children—a calling that led to a rewarding and meaningful career.

As a new author, Sylvia draws inspiration from both her professional experiences and her own childhood, crafting heartfelt and relatable stories for children. Her work celebrates the beauty, challenges, and joy of growing up, and reflects her deep commitment to the well-being and development of every child.

www.ingramcontent.com/pod-product-compliance
Lightning Source LLC
Chambersburg PA
CBHW041135120626
46547CB00019B/2997